Dealing With Your Kids' 7 Biggest Troubles

Also from Boys Town Press

For Parents

Common Sense Parenting® (also in audio and Spanish)

Common Sense Parenting Learn-at-Home Video Kit

Angry Kids, Frustrated Parents

Boys Town Videos for Parents

Parents and Kids Talking About Preventing Violence

Unmasking Sexual Con Games: Parent Guide

Getting Along with Others: Activity Book

For Teens

A Good Friend: How to Make One, How to Be One

Who's in the Mirror? Finding the Real Me

*What's Right for Me? Making Good
    Choices in Relationships*

*One to One: Listening Tapes on Dating,
    Alcohol, Suicide and More*

Unmasking Sexual Con Games: Student Guide

**For a free Boys Town Press catalog,
call 1-800-282-6657**.

A BOYS TOWN
How-To Book

Dealing With Your Kids' 7 Biggest Troubles

**Lying, Cheating, Stealing, Sexual
Acting Out, Drugs & Alcohol,
Suicide, Violence**

Val J. Peter
Executive Director, Boys Town

BOYS
TOWN
PRESS

Dealing With Your Kids' 7 Biggest Troubles

Published by the Boys Town Press
Father Flanagan's Boys' Home
Boys Town, Nebraska 68010

Publisher's Cataloging in Publication
(Prepared by Quality Books Inc.)

Peter, Val J.
      Dealing with your kids' 7 biggest troubles : a Boys Town how-to book / Val J. Peter. --1st ed.
      p. cm.
      ISBN: 0-938510-97-5

      1. Child rearing. 2. Parent and teenager.
3. Adolescent psychology. I. Title.

HQ796.P48 2000   649'.125
                          QBI99-1604

10   9   8   7   6   5   4   3   2

*Parents and children can
call the Boys Town National Hotline
for help with any problem,
24 hours a day, every day.*

Table of Contents

Introduction

More than anything else, kids want love and acceptance. They want to feel they are in charge of their lives, while at the same time knowing they can rely on trustworthy adults.

There are seven major obstacles to feeling accepted and loved. They are:

1. Lying
2. Cheating

3. Stealing

4. Inappropriate Sexual Behavior

5. Drugs and Alcohol

6. Suicide

7. Violence

Parents and teachers and other mentors can help kids overcome these seven obstacles. How?

■ By role modeling appropriate behavior.

■ By teaching appropriate behavior.

■ By reinforcing appropriate behavior.

The purpose of this little book is to provide guidance so that you can help kids achieve these very, very important goals in their young lives. Please read this book slowly and share it with others. We at Boys Town have found the suggestions made here have provided us guidance as we help our boys and girls move toward happy, productive lives.

Where do kids learn how to lie, cheat, and steal? They don't make it up themselves. They learn it from others. Not only their peers, but even their teachers and their parents.

- John is one of my boys who was caught shoplifting the other day. I asked him who taught him how to steal. He said his dad did. His dad told him: "Stores make a 10% allowance for shoplifting. And we just want to get our share." You and I can help John.

- Martha is one of our girls who had a very bad habit of lying to try to avoid responsibility for inappropriate behaviors. I asked her who taught her to lie. She said: "My mom lied to my dad all the time when she was cheating on him. And she got away with it. So I thought I would try it, too."

You and I can help kids move away from harmful behaviors. By doing so, we will help them have a much more happy childhood and adolescence. A truthful, honest child is a joy indeed.

A how-to book such as this can not only help your children, but it can help you be better parents as well. There are a lot of reasons why children lie to their moms and dads. One reason has to do with punishment. If parents punish too severely and too frequently, the child will often develop the habit of lying to mom and dad to avoid too-severe punishment. In that case, a good mom and dad make appropriate adjustments in the kind of negative consequences they mete out.

On the other hand, children sometimes learn to lie to avoid any consequences whatsoever. Did you ever ask an explanation of your 16-year-old son as to why he came home at 3 a.m. Sunday morning instead of midnight? His first response won't necessarily be the fullness of truth. Here, too, we can help our children learn that truth telling is rewarded in some significant way.

Helping a child feel good when he or she tells the truth is helping a child develop a conscience. You are also helping a child develop a conscience when you give him or her a negative consequence for lying.

What a blessing it is for children who have parents who help form their conscience. A person with a well-formed conscience has a far, far greater chance of happiness in this life – and heaven, too!

Liar, Liar, Pants on Fire

Nobody likes a liar. Nobody wants their children to grow up to be liars. How can you help your son or daughter cherish truth-telling?

Role
Modeling

Don't teach your kids to lie.

It's pretty clear you're "teaching" your son to lie when you ask him to "cover for you" with your spouse. For example, Mom tells Billy: "When Dad asks what happened to his fishing rod, don't tell him I stepped on it. Tell him the dog sat on it and broke it." Or Dad tells Maria: "If Mom asks you whether I talked to Grandma about the fight we had, tell her no." Another way to teach your children to lie is to brag about how you told your boss a big story to get yourself off the hook when you messed up at work. "Your dad is no sucker, son."

It's very common today, for example, for a child to get into trouble at school for fighting. The parents get involved, and Mom or Dad teach the child how to lie to get out of it: "Actually, Johnny started the fight, not me. I was only defending myself." Or two kids talk to each other: "I don't have to worry about my school behavior. My dad will hire a lawyer and sue the school."

All of those are pretty clear ways that parents literally teach their children to lie. There is another way that is more subtle.

Overpunishment

If parents overpunish a child when he or she does something wrong, they are teaching the child to lie. Lying becomes an escape response, which to a child, seems preferable to the overpunishment of a physical beating or a parental tirade that goes on and on. Parents need to be more helpers than punishers, and our children need to see that.

When our children get themselves into trouble, that's the time to teach rather than just punish. Don't get me wrong. I am not advocating letting your kids get away with things. I am saying just the opposite. Don't let them get away with anything. But also, don't overpunish. Teach them, teach them, teach them. Some punishment is necessary. You bet. But throwing fits or punches will not help your child develop a conscience about truth-telling.

When you catch your child in a lie, you have a great opportunity to help his or her conscience develop. You see, lying isn't just a behavioral thing. It's a spiritual thing. Morally good people are honest. They really are.

What *Lying* Does

There are four things to discuss with your child when he or she is caught in a big lie:

■ People don't like liars. They don't like to be with them. They don't like to talk with them. They don't like to do business with them. They don't like to socialize with them. They just don't like liars.

- God doesn't like lying. The serpent lied to Eve. The devil is the father of lies. Jesus told us, "You will know the truth, and the truth will set you free."

- Third, the human body itself does not like lying. Think about a lie detector test when a person's body itself can say, "I am lying." Even our bodies are built to pay the consequences of lying by nervous reactions recordable on a graph.

- Finally, you lose people's trust when you lie. Tell your son that when he lies he loses your trust. Losing a parent's or teacher's trust is a high price to pay. Parents are disappointed. They are hurt. Remind your daughter that when she catches her friend telling a lie that she loses a little bit of trust in that friend as well.

The Lord has created us in such a way that we have to pay the consequences for lying. People don't like us. We lose their trust. We don't like ourselves. It's hard to keep friends. Our conscience tells us we've done wrong. God wants the truth, not lies.

This is a good time to let your sons and daughters know that when they lie they need to confess their sins to the Lord. If there is real sorrow in our hearts and a desire not to lie again, the Lord forgives us and restores us because He loves us. Remind your child how to "fix" a lie by telling the truth and making "restitution" for the lie. The remedy for sin is repentance.

Lies, Errors, *and* Stories

There is a difference between a lie, an error, and a fanciful story. If a child says

$2 + 2 = 5$, that's not a lie or a fanciful story. It's an error. The remedy for that error is education, namely an extra math lesson.

Fanciful stories that are told in the context of love and trust are cherished by all. Santa Claus is such a fanciful story. It's not an error. It's not a lie. Ask your children, both those who are young and those who are older, and they will tell you the truth about the beauty of Santa Claus. (The Easter Bunny just can't hold a candle to Santa Claus, in my opinion, even if the rabbit is still a good fanciful story.)

However, when we try to distort who we are and what we do, that's a lie, not an error or a fanciful story. Lies are destructive. With addictions, lies become a way of life. So, too, with affairs and pretty soon life itself becomes a lie.

Many reformed liars will tell you how much better life is now that they practice the truth. They don't have to keep track of their lies, trying to remember from person to person and place to place what "lie" they used the last time. A liar can never "relax" and really enjoy life because there is always the danger of exposure and getting caught.

I hope your child learns truth-telling skills. Just as there are skills you need to be a good liar, so there are skills you need to tell the truth. Teach your children how to tell the truth, how to love the truth, how to share the truth. Help them understand truth is not a weapon to hurt other people. Only cynics do that.

One final thought. In politics, truth has never been popular. Teach your children that truth is very important and very popular in your family. Tell them, "We don't care how many lies politicians tell. We don't lie in this family." Show your children how beautiful truth is.

Truth really is luminous whether it be a truth of physics or a personal truth. And the greatest truth is: "I love you."

Nobody Likes a *Cheat*

In movie Westerns, a cowboy who cheats at cards is usually shot right then and there. The sheriff doesn't intervene. That's frontier justice.

Nobody likes a cheat. Yet we live in a society known for getting around the rules. We all know what cheating is:

- Not following the rules.
- Using other people's homework in school.

- Copying answers during tests.

- Cheating at cards.

- Cheating at games.

- Cheating in sports events.

- Just plain dishonesty.

How do we teach our children not to cheat? How do we teach them honesty?

Teaching *Honesty*

Don't let your children learn cheating from you.

It is pretty obvious that if you cheat, (on your expense account, your golf score, your spouse), your children will grow up to be cheats. The contrary is also true. If you don't cheat and make every effort to teach your children that cheating is wrong, your children will grow up to be honest people. (I had a friend who cheated at everything. My parents' heated and repeated expressions of disapproval heightened within me my awareness of the importance of being honest.)

Watch out for parenting strategies that make cheating attractive to your children:

- Avoid unreasonable expectations about your children's grades in school.

- Why? Because unreasonable expectations can create conditions that make cheating an acceptable behavior to your child.

- Your child might think, "I'd rather get a good grade by cheating than be honest, get a poor grade, and have to face the wrath of my parents."

Think of the pressure you put on your children via this parenting strategy:

- "Everyone in this family goes to Harvard."

- "I won't accept a stupid child."

- Of course, you don't want your children to be lazy.

- The remedy for laziness is a series of positive and negative motivations served up with warmth and affection and stick-to-itiveness.

- If your child is lazy in school, get involved in his schoolwork.

- Meet with teachers who can help give you a realistic assessment of your child's potential.

- Use sports as an example. Most parents who attend their children's sporting events realize their children are not future NBA or NFL players.

- These are realistic expectations. They need to prevail in academics as well.

When Your Child *Cheats*

What to do when your child is caught cheating on a test:

- The first thing that you need to do is to get the facts: "Is this the first event?" "Has it been going on for some time?" "Was it a prank?" "Was it serious?" "Was it peer pressure?"

- In addition to getting the facts, it is important to control your own emotions. There is a sizable difference between a disappointment and a disaster. Parents need to recognize that and communicate it to their children. It is a disappointment that your child was cheating on a test, but it is not the end of the world.

■ Third, in addition to getting the facts and controlling your own emotions, it is important to find out what the pressures are on your child to cheat. Then help reduce those pressures.

Using these three simple steps usually produces an abundance of insights as to how to handle the situation. Usually your child will feel very embarrassed and ashamed. That is a great time to show a parent's love, especially true if your child has "come to his senses." (I like that phrase. Luke uses it to describe the Prodigal son. It motivated the Prodigal son to confess. "I have sinned against heaven and you, Father.")

This presents you with an opportunity to give your child a big hug and not hold a grudge. "To err is human. To forgive is divine."

Sometimes, you will be surprised at what motivates your child to cheat. For example, boys from about age 10 to 14 tend to enter into little groups which engage in forbidden activities such as cheating or shoplifting that bond the group together. Forbidden activities are part of a developmental process in which pre-adolescents make symbolic departures away from their moms and dads before actually doing so.

You as a parent have to put an end to these illicit thrills. There are lots of appropriate thrills that kids can engage in.

Nobody likes a cheat. Teach your kids not to get into card games where they have to cheat to win.

Teaching Children About Stealing: *Childhood*

We need to teach our children not to steal. In the process, parents can help develop a growing sense of justice in their children.

Justice is the bedrock of civilization. Justice is the least we can do for one another. Without justice, human togetherness is impossible. The most we can do for one another is love each other.

A Sense of *Justice*

This occurs very early in life, when little children, about 2 years old, discover that they are not the center of the universe. This is a far-reaching discovery for a child. Part of it is the realization that "not all toys in the world belong to me." This comes as a surprise to a child entering the terrible two's.

At this stage, children do not steal as much as they pick up things that don't belong to them and walk off. When a child's mother says: "That doll belongs to your sister you need to give it back," here begins an incipient notion of justice in the child. It is the notion: "Things belong to people, and I cannot take them."

Little Jimmy, age 2, does not understand it right now, but this notion that his sister's toys belong to her is the beginning of the realization that his sister has value and worth as a fellow member of the human family. It is the beginning of the process of recognizing our common humanity. This won't be clear to Jimmy now. But later on as he grows, it will become very clear.

Stealing

As Jimmy begins to grow and develop, his parents help him understand that it is not only wrong to take what belongs to his sister, he also discovers that he needs to give it back to her. He may think that this is only because she is his sister and a member of his family. He loves her. Soon he discovers that he cannot take the toys of his neighbors either. He also cannot take toys from a store or school whenever he feels like it. This is another major step on the way to becoming a just person.

Jimmy will learn that even if he will never see someone again, he cannot steal from that person. Even if the person is a stranger or someone he doesn't like, he cannot steal from him or her.

If children see their parents stealing, then it is very likely that this will be an encouragement for the children to try it themselves. Children mimic parents in ways that are sometimes a surprise to the parents.

For example, a third-grade teacher told me about an exercise for math in which she was teaching a mantra to her students: "Two and two, the sum of which is four; three and three, the sum of which is six. One boy was not saying it that way. He was saying: "Two and two, the son of a b---- is four; three and three, the son of a b----- is six." The boy obviously did not make that phrase up, but learned it from his father or some other adult.

Bullying

When a young child runs into a bully, it often is his or her first experience with an unjust world.

The child meets a bully at school who takes his lunch money or candy money by force:

- It is a formative experience for the child.

- The child is unable to express it adequately because such a thing never happened at home.

- There were failures of family sharing at home, like a brother taking a bite out of your cake and running.

But here we have the techniques of a bully:

- "If you don't give me your lunch money, I will hurt you."

- "If you tell anyone, I will hurt you worse."

- This is the child's first experience of the world as an unjust place. It is forced on him by a bully who says: "I want to hurt you, frighten you, and dominate you. I want the thing you have."

- It is a formative experience to understand that the ways of the world include even this.

- "What I see on TV," says the child, "happens even in my own life."

- That child's reaction is emotional: "This is not fair."

- Think of all the minority children who face prejudice for the first time.

Here a child has the opportunity to learn adaptation skills:

- A child needs to learn to respect other people's property, even if other people do not respect his or hers.

■ A child needs to learn to tell his or her parents in the hope that they can help or tell the police.

■ A child learns to move right on from this and not dwell on it. Mom or Dad needs to teach their child how to do this, namely, move on from the experience and not be traumatized by it.

The child learns a "do" list and a "don't" list. In the child's "do" list, he or she learns:

■ Avoid things that make you an easy target.

■ Confront behavior if it will have good consequences.

■ Have others such as your parents or the police confront the behavior.

In the "don't" list, a child learns:

■ Don't escalate the violence.

■ Don't start a fight that you are going to lose.

- Don't irritate a bull or wake a sleeping dragon.

- Don't look for trouble.

The goal here is to come to an understanding of how to deal with injustice in the world.

- A wrong conclusion is: "I am personally incompetent to live in the world."

- Another inappropriate conclusion: "I deny the trouble exists, so I run away and I do not go to school anymore."

Shoplifting

As a little boy or girl begins to grow, he or she sees shoplifting for the first time in their lives. Most of us can remember that day and describe it rather vividly. It makes a big impression.

How much bigger an impression it makes if you see your brother or your sister shoplifting. It makes an even bigger impression if you see your mother or your father shoplifting. We have a boy here at Boys Town with a bad habit of shoplifting. He is following the example of his father, who told him: "Stores have a 10 percent allowance for shoplifting. I just need to get my share of the 10 percent."

When a child is caught stealing or shoplifting, three things are in order:

■ **Make an apology.** This should be a face-to-face encounter with the person from whom the goods were stolen. Make it a public event in contrast to stealing or shoplifting which is always a private event.

■ **Make restitution.** If I steal $50 from you, it is not sufficient to tell you that I am sorry. You are going to honestly ask:

"Where is my $50?" Restitution means making up for the bad example I gave my peers.

■ **Ask the Lord's forgiveness.** The third thing a thief needs to do is to make an apology and restitution to the good Lord Himself. Until I kneel in humility before the Lord and acknowledge that this is not a mistake but a sin, I will still think of it as akin to going over the speed limit. In other words, I think of it as something society says we should not do, but "most everybody does anyway."

Repetitive *Stealing*

What if a boy or girl is caught shoplifting, not just once, but three, four, or five times?

The problem we are talking about transitions us from stealing in childhood to stealing in adolescence.

Politicians and talk show commentators usually start at this point. They want to know what is to be done with a person who is turning into a thief.

It should be clear that when a boy steals for the first time he is not buying into his parents' values of respect for the rights of others. In addition to an apology and restitution, a number of processes need to be put in place including:

- Certain friends are off-limits.

- Certain situations where stealing is so attractive need to be avoided.

- The "thrill" of stealing needs to be replaced with something equally rewarding. What is it that can replace this materialism and this disrespect for the rights of others? The most power-

ful and rewarding replacement is
relationships. How about Dad saying:
"Son, I'd like to spend some time with
you this weekend at a movie or going
bowling or hiking."

It is in this situation where the churches
and synagogues need to come into play.

- If certain friends are off-limits, are
  there church groups which might
  present an attractive, welcoming experience for a young boy who is confused
  but open to positive relationships?

- Similarly, service experiences (serving
  meals to the homeless, visiting the sick)
  are relationship-building. You are not
  trying to frustrate the young man's
  desire to get his needs met. You are
  trying to show him that he can get his
  needs met in a prosocial way rather
  than in an antisocial way.

A child caught shoplifting three times, however, should be turned over to the law. Hopefully, the judge will put the child on probation.

Here is where the politician enters in and is tempted to use marketing strategies that end up being nothing more than superstitious beliefs. People then begin to vote their anger instead of voting their hopes, and to feel better about something getting done. Even though in the end, things are as bad if not worse.

Diversion programs do not end delinquency. Not because the logic is flawed, but because some kids need constant external control of their environment until they change – until a reinforcer comes into their life which helps them to change.

Boot camps do not end delinquency. Not because the logic is flawed, but because certain youngsters need constant external control

until they change. That's right, until a reinforcer comes into their lives. Here are some
examples of reinforcers for young people:

- Perhaps they fall in love.

- Perhaps they get a job they really like.

- Perhaps they are touched by a kind
  person.

- Perhaps they discover that they have a
  certain potential.

It is important at this point to realize that
time is definitely on your side. Everybody is
looking for a quick fix. In situations that we
are describing here, there is no quick fix.

What Parents
Can Do

When you look at the issue of teaching
respect for the rights of others from age 2 on,

there are three imperatives which apply in every age in an age-appropriate way and which are the keys to success:

- ■ "Tell it." (This is teaching skills such as honesty.)

- ■ "Model it." (This is building relationships with your child.)

- ■ "Monitor it." (This is a combination of skills in relationships and feedback.)

A free society cannot flourish without private virtue. The common good is dependent upon parents teaching, modeling, and monitoring in age-appropriate ways, in order to pass on to children respect for the rights of others. Any public policy that neglects these will do so to its own regret.

Protecting the rights of others is the minimum manifestation of human togetherness that is needed for human flourishing. In other words, respecting the rights of others is the least we can do for one another. And love is the most.

Justice is the cornerstone of human beings living together in peace. Justice is a journey, and one of the secrets of success on the journey is how to live in a world which is not always fair to you, your children, or others. The family is the first teacher of justice, the place where youngsters can take encouragement to "not be overcome by evil, but overcome evil by doing good."

Thou Shalt Not Steal:
Adolescence & Adulthood

Instilling a sense of justice in our children starts early on. But it takes on a new importance in adolescence.

When the people of Israel came to Mount Sinai, they were asked if they wanted to be the people of God. If they did, the Lord told them, one of the main things they would have to do is not to steal from anyone at all. Not just from their sister or brother whom they loved, but they could not steal from neighbors. They could not steal from strangers. They could not steal from shops or schools or anyplace. Stealing was something they could not do and still be members of God's holy people.

- If you live in a house where everybody steals from everybody else, it is not possible for that house to become a home.

- If you live in a house where everybody steals from everybody else, you will put a padlock on both your possessions and your heart.

Why do people steal? Because stealing gets you something that you want.

- A child says to his or her mother: "I want a candy bar."

- She says: "No, you can't have one."

- The child either learns the adjustment skill of how to take "no" for an answer or the child looks at stealing as a solution.

Taking "no" for an answer is a step toward a more just world. Stealing is a step toward a more unjust world.

It is in adolescence that kids are introduced to issues of justice and fair labor practices. This is more complicated than shoplifting.

Fair Labor Practices

One of the first things a boy or girl with a first job realizes is that "the laborer is worthy of his hire."

- A 16-year-old goes to work at a fast food restaurant.

- The restaurant promises to pay her $7.50 an hour.

- She works 40 hours, and they pay her for only 38 hours.

■ That is unjust.

■ There are many unfair labor practices that an adolescent may run into.

This teen has an opportunity to grow further in the ways of justice. She needs to learn to find ways to appropriately seek redress for what she has been unjustly deprived of.

The other side of fair labor practices is the worker cheating his boss, cheating the company he works for.

■ A 16-year-old in his first job is working for a fast food restaurant.

■ He gets somebody else to punch the time clock for him for two hours that he did not work.

■ He is stealing from his employer.

Both situations are tough for 16-year-olds to accept. They are not 2-year-olds anymore taking a sister's toys or having another snatch theirs. They are becoming persons of maturity and understanding, and with maturity comes additional opportunities and responsibilities for making the world a more just place.

Justice and Persons in *Terrible Need*

If I have adequate food and someone is starving, do I, in justice, need to share some food with them? Do I, in justice, have to share some of my hard-earned money from my first job?

- The answer is yes.

- This is a giant step forward toward a more just world.

- It is as big as the step of a 2-year-old giving his sister's doll back.

- This is a painful stepping away from complete selfishness.

- I really owe someone based on extreme need because he or she is my brother or sister.

- Even if it is a complete stranger, I owe it to him or her.

What if a child is born physically or mentally challenged? Do we as taxpayers have to pay extra so that the public schools will provide special education for these children or special accommodations for their physical disabilities?

The answer is yes. It is a matter of justice. As you can see, this is another gigantic step forward toward a more just world.

Listen to our selfish thoughts:

- "It is my money, and I can do with it as I want."

- "It is my hard-earned money, and they didn't earn it. Why do you say that I have to give them some of it?"

- "It is not my fault they are handicapped."

- "If I give, it will be out of charity, not justice."

- "I don't owe them anything."

As you can see, it is a giant step forward when we realize in our hearts that we owe that starving person out of justice.

Boys and girls have to pray awfully hard to have this message touch their souls. They have to get to the point where the relationship with their heavenly Father is very strong. They must come to realize in their hearts that we are all brothers and sisters. As the Lord says: "I was hungry, and you gave me something to eat."

Most requests you and I receive are, however, for donations from people who are not starving. They are requesting works of charity. We should not exaggerate the demands of justice.

Disrespecting Women and Minorities

What have we learned about justice?

■ As a 2-year-old, we gave our sister her toy back because it was hers and not ours.

■ As we grew a little older, we realized that shoplifting was wrong and how important it is that we do not steal from one another, even those whom we do not know.

■ We also begin to realize that we must be fair with each other in business as customers, as laborers, and as merchants.

■ Then we began to realize that out of justice we need to give to someone in dire need just because they are in dire need and even if he or she did not earn it.

Now we are going to take a giant step forward and understand something even more important.

■ Justice isn't just about playthings or items in the store.

■ It isn't just about wages.

■ It isn't just about being hungry.

■ Justice is about being brothers and sisters to one another.

■ Justice is realizing that all of us are related to our heavenly Father.

■ Justice is about treating each other like the brothers and sisters that we are.

■ It is about treating each other as children of our heavenly Father.

■ It is like beginning to understand that just as in our families we cannot steal and still be a family, neither can we disrespect minorities and be brothers and sisters to each other.

■ Neither can we disrespect women and be brothers and sisters to each other.

Why is this so hard to see? Because of selfishness.

What is this prejudice about? It's about self-absorption, isolation, and power.

Each one of us needs to make a personal response as we face these challenges to our moral and religious development.

I like to suggest to our kids here at Boys Town that we begin by looking at the crucifix with the Easter winding cloths draped upon it:

■ Start this meditation by contemplating the death and resurrection of Jesus for our salvation.

- It is Jesus putting justice back into the world and filling it with love.

- We need to be His hands and His heart in the world.

- Putting justice back is the bedrock of all civilization.

- His followers need to be just by not taking from their brothers and sisters what belongs to them.

- His followers need to be just by not stealing from strangers or stores.

- His followers need to be just by not stealing from workers or being unfair to them.

- His followers need to be just by giving an honest day's labor and not ripping off their employers.

- His followers need to be just by giving to those in dire need. His followers need to be just by treating minorities and women with equality.

■ His followers need not only to be just (which is the least they can do), but also to be loving (which is the most they can do).

The winding cloths on the crucifix indicate that the Lord has risen and sent His Spirit into our midst. We have the power to do this if we will only develop a personal relationship with Jesus Christ and with His saving community, the Church.

Your Teenager and Sex

One of the seven great scourges of adolescence is sexual acting out. There is no bigger topic than this for your teenager.

Let's look at three factors.

Desensitization

Desensitization to sex has already happened to your child.

Any good parent in America today knows that adolescence is a quicksand that easily envelops the unwary. Because it is a sexually toxic world, parents have often resorted to made-up stories to keep their children out of harm's way:

- If you have sex, you'll ruin your life forever.

- If you play with yourself, you'll go blind.

- If you have sex once, you'll get AIDS and are sure to die.

- If you have sex twice, everyone will think you're a "ho."

These are unbelievable stories. In our day and age, they don't work. In fact, by debunking these unrealistic taboos the media have swept all moral norms away, even the vital and most important ones:

- God created sexual intimacy for the committed love relationship of marriage.

- Putting sex anywhere outside of marriage is morally wrong: harmful to self, the other, and the whole community.

The first step then is desensitization.

Experimentation

Once all the taboos and commandments have been swept away, the second step (to fill the void) is a call to experimentation. The gurus of sexual liberation do this well:

- Young (fourth and fifth grade) kids are told to "begin your sexual awakening."

- That is followed by the admonition to "explore your sexuality."

- Boys are told: "It's okay to force your girlfriend to have sex if you have been dating at least six months."

- Girls are told: "Give him what he wants and keep him happy. If you don't have a boyfriend, you're nothing."

■ But girls are also told: "Don't get pregnant."

■ Therefore, protected sex is a responsible option.

All of these are recipes for disaster. A young girl's or boy's body is not an amusement park. It's a temple of the Holy Spirit.

Taboos

Early on, parents have to do a lot of teaching and set up solid rules.

In order to inculcate God's good rules about marriage and family, parents need to be very specific about their teaching and their rules:

■ I like to call these rules taboos that are healthy and helpful. They are God's good commandments.

- A good taboo is something "we just don't do no matter what" because it destroys our lives and our ability to live in union with God and others in God.

When it comes to your head, you know right away what not to do:

- Incest, no matter how consensual, is a taboo.

- Trying to force your girlfriend of six months to have sex is a taboo.

- Hitting a girl with disrespect is a taboo.

- Giving a guy some head is a taboo.

These should not only sound awful, they should elicit awful feelings.

- All of these are harmful to self, others, and the community.

- They are sinful and hurtful.

- God created sex for marriage and nowhere else.

Your church, your school, and the friends that parents run around with all need to reinforce these rules.

If you yell at your children for lying and then at supper you brag about pulling the wool over your boss's eyes, you're teaching them to lie. Actions speak louder than words. You can do the same thing with sex: "You aren't 18 yet."

On the other hand, prudishness won't help either. How many parents, who when their child gets into the fifth or sixth grade, suddenly become prudes? Your children can see right through that.

A Child's *Moral* Pattern

The boy-girl relations your child develops will be highly impacted by his or her younger years.

It is important to understand this. When sexual awakening arrives it is folded into the general moral pattern of your child's behavior.

If your child has developed the capacity for healthy friendships among peers when younger, it will be easier to continue this into the dating scene. The best preparation for marriage and family is to develop the capacity for friendship between boys and girls.

- If you and your child have developed the ability to talk to each other when younger, it will be easier to continue this into the dating scene.

- If your child has developed the capacity for friendship and prayer with the Lord, it will be easier to carry this over when he or she begins to date.

- If your young child has developed habits of lying, cheating, and stealing, sex will just be another area in which to lie, cheat, and steal when puberty arrives.

■ If your child has developed unhealthy patterns of guilt and self-blame when younger, it will be easier to carry this over into the dating scene.

■ If, however, your child has avoided lying, cheating, and stealing, sexual awakening will still be a period of great temptation to lie, cheat, and steal via sex, but the odds are in favor of more honesty and less self-deception.

And just as with lying, cheating, and stealing, the best approach in teaching is not exclusively a religious one, but a combination of secular and religious wisdom. So, too, here with sexual behavior.

In the end, stand firm, stand tall, and stand together.

Experimentation with Drugs and Alcohol

Your son is 14 years old. You just found out five minutes ago that he is involved with marijuana. He tells you, "I smoked some weed once or twice. Don't get your feathers ruffled." But it hits you like a ton of bricks: The enemy is not at the door. The enemy is inside your house.

What are you going to do? The first two or three days after this shocking discovery are the most important.

The thought that may come to your mind is, "Why me? Why us? What have we done to deserve this?" You are upset. You are hurt. You are ashamed and angry. You are disappointed. You think: "What are people going to say about us? What is going to happen to us as a family?"

Dealing with Your *Fears*

You may react to these feelings of pain in one of two ways – by "minimizing" or "maximizing." For example, you might be tempted to minimize by telling yourself:

■ "He only smoked once."

■ "It's only a passing episode."

■ "He just did it to fit in."

■ "Every kid experiments with drugs."

- "He'll never do it again."

- "He's such a good boy."

On the other hand, you might be tempted to maximize your fears:

- "My son's going to become a street-level addict."

- "He is doomed to OD and die."

- "He needs to be packed off to Switzerland to a treatment institute."

- "He's probably a dealer, too."

Instead of doing either, first get yourself under control. You need to stay calm. What does that mean?

- Go into your bedroom. Have a good cry.

- Don't talk to your son until your emotions are under control.

- If you're upset for an hour or two, go to church.

- Get in touch with your faith, your trust in the Lord. The faith walk begins right now.

- There's an old adage: "Never try to teach a drunk." This is equally true if drugs are still coursing through his veins.

Spend as much time as you need to get this done. Your spouse needs to do the same. Tell your son: "Give me some time. My emotions are running wild."

Communicating with Your Teen

Next, you need to start talking. This is critical. By now you are somewhat calmed down. But a paradox presents itself: You want open and honest communication, but you don't believe a thing your son says. Or you are tempted to engage in a CIA operation (bug the phone, hire a private detective, and other covert operations) or mimic the Gestapo ("We have ways of making you talk").

The most important thing to remember at this point is that truth-telling is a process. That means the first time your son talks he will tell you about 10 percent of what is going on. In many cases, he's not lying. He's just telling you some things about his life. Not many, but some. Once again, truth-telling is a process and takes time.

The second or third time you talk, you can begin asking questions that gain more and more information. You will probably learn about peer pressure in your son's life. He may tell you:

- "My friends are all using."

- "It's fun to use."

- "I want to fit in and belong."

- "What's the big deal? Didn't you try drugs when you were a kid?"

- "It's fun to test the rules and take risks."

Examining
the Family

Then you have to ask yourself other questions that are a little harder:

- What are the dynamics in our family?

- What are our parenting styles?

- What is our role modeling like? Are we using alcohol, prescription or other drugs as a way to deal with stress or in excessive amounts?

- Is our son playing one of us against the other?

It's important, too, to ask yourselves as parents how you have settled serious issues in the past with your child. If you have settled things in a healthy fashion before, your son will remember that. This should give both of you the courage to tackle this problem together.

It is also good to remember that the community you live in is also predictive of drug usage. The more adults who do not disapprove of marijuana usage in a community, the higher the percentage it will have of youngsters who will experiment. That's why growing up in Southern California is more difficult than growing up in Peoria. Parents in different communities may have different challenges in working with their children.

Taking *Action*

Here are some things you should do right away:

- Check at school to see if there are problems with your son's behavior or academic work.

- Find out who his friends are.

■ Check on how your son is spending his money and where it comes from.

What you're looking for is whether your son is involved in experimental or patterned drug usage. If it's experimental use and your son is willing to work with you, you have real chances for success, provided you can get yourself under control and start a dialogue with him. You will probably find the truth somewhere between maximizing and minimizing what is going on.

It is time now for action and for setting up consequences. Here are some steps you need to take:

■ **More frequent communication** with your son.

■ **More vigilance** – watching for signs of drug use or drug paraphernalia.

■ **More monitoring** – which friends is he spending time with and what are they doing.

- **More accountability** – setting up consequences for things like skipping school or hanging out with kids known to be involved with drugs.

- **More positive interaction** with your son, too – planning activities you both can enjoy, praising the good things he does.

In the end, it is our faith life that tips the balance in favor of healing and hope. "Those who trust in the Lord are not disappointed."

How to
Handle Teenage
Addiction

In the previous chapter, we talked about teenagers' experimentation with drugs and alcohol. Now comes the far tougher topic of how to help parents deal with the disease of addiction in the life of their teenager.

If a teen has moved from experimentation to the disease stage, then there is a huge need for parents to adjust. They need to move away from their adolescent's past misbehavior that was influenced by peers and friends to dealing with a disease process that takes on a life of its own. Their adolescent has crossed that line. The progressive disease of addiction is now present.

Denial **and Delay**

The reality of habitual use usually hits parents between the eyes only because some calamitous event occurs in their teen's life. Perhaps your son was arrested for DWI or was picked up at K-Mart for trying to return stolen goods. Or your daughter quit school. Or you found some nasty looking pills in her jeans pocket. When that happens, parents start putting together other noticeable changes in their teenager's life:

- Erratic behavior

- Too much or too little sleep

- Not eating regularly

- Highs and lows/mood swings
- A drop in grades or dropping out of school
- Secretive or hiding behavior
- Decline in physical appearance
- A change in friends
- Gone for long periods of time
- Strange phone calls

None of these symptoms by itself is proof positive. But a pattern of them suggests that your child needs a chemical dependency evaluation. This is an important step.

- You won't find out by having a conversation with your teen.
- You won't find out by asking opinions of people at the office or even by asking the family physician.
- The best person to consult is a certified chemical dependency counselor.

Where do you find one of those? Check in the phone book or call the Boys Town National Hotline at 1-800-448-3000 for a referral.

You as a parent will be tempted to delay. You may tell yourself:

■ "All she needs is a little rest."

■ "We'll wait 'til school is over."

■ "Summer in the Catskills will change everything."

■ "We'll have him talk to Father Smith at the parish."

None of these is a real fix for the progressive disease of addiction. Yes, alcohol experimentation is part of growing up. And yes, sowing one's wild oats or going through a rebellious stage is sometimes a part of adolescence. But people don't "grow out" of addiction; they just get worse. If intervention occurs, however, a teen can begin to recover from it.

This disease is characterized by denial. The person who has it believes he doesn't. The person who has it says: "I want to be good and engage in appropriate behavior. This is not a problem. I can handle it." But he doesn't, and he can't. He is powerless before the disease.

The denial part of the disease makes your teenager full of excuses and ready to blame. It's always somebody else's fault, and there is always an excuse for every missed step. She denies she is in denial. She will look you straight in the eye and say all she knows about "denial" is that "it's a river in Egypt."

Wrong **Routes**

Parents are susceptible to the extremes of anger and pity. You are hurt. You are ashamed. You are disappointed. The anger is easy to understand: "Our child's behavior is shameful. How could he (or she) do this to us? What are people going to say?"

Or there is pity. What caused "our poor child" to fall into this trouble? Parents can become "enablers." They participate in the denial themselves which enables the addicted teen to avoid getting help.

A person who has used alcohol or drugs a lot will experience a physiological process of withdrawal. It's really not like the delirium seen in the movies. But, the shaking, sweating, nausea, and terrible anxiety will make it hard to talk to your teen during this process.

I like to stress the "six don'ts" that parents should follow at this time:

- Don't rescue. Your child is responsible for his or her recovery.

- Don't be inconsistent in your plan.

■ Don't let your teen divide and conquer you as parents.

■ Don't accept responsibility for your child's behavior. You are responsible for your behavior, not his or hers.

■ Don't expect instant results.

■ Don't give up, quit, or be fatalistic.

What You *Should Do*

Can you search your teen's room for evidence of drug use? Of course. This is justifiable paternalism. If your son or daughter was standing on a bridge ready to jump, wouldn't you be justified as a parent in grabbing and stopping him or her? Of course.

But is this a denial of the teen's freedom? Absolutely not. Anyone who has stopped another from committing suicide knows that as the person gets better, he or she will thank the rescuer. Your teen will not thank you now. It will take a long time; but it will happen.

What should you say to your child? First, don't talk when he or she is drunk or high on drugs. Pick a time when your teen is feeling sick. He or she is more vulnerable then. You will have better results. You should:

- Confront your teen's behavior. Say, "You have a problem."

- Prepare for denial.

- Insist on a chemical dependency evaluation.

- Do this together as a family if you can.

If the evaluation determines that treatment is needed, there are three possibilities:

- Inpatient care

- Day treatment

- Outpatient care

Severity of the problem should be the criterion for the type of treatment you choose, but more often than not, money is. In any treatment, parents need to realize that their participation is part and parcel of the road to recovery.

It is my firm conviction that the Twelve-Step program of Alcoholics Anonymous provides the single, most consistent opportunity for a person to get better and move positively into recovery. If, after treatment, a teenager does not attend meetings and, just as importantly, does not have a sponsor, then prepare yourself for more trouble. Also, keep in mind that, on average, a chemically dependent person has to go through treatment three times before there are substantial results.

That shouldn't be a discouragement. It should be an encouragement to start now.

Taking *Care* of Yourself

The addiction process has already taken its toll on you as parents. So take the following steps:

- Turn to those who love you. Don't go it alone.

- Turn especially to "the Lord, who is my strength and my salvation."

- Resist the temptation to react to setbacks and disappointments too quickly and recklessly.

- The disease has affected you. Alanon is a powerful support group. Join now.

When I think of all the Boys Town kids in recovery and how happy they are, I know there is hope.

Teaching Kids About Suicide

Parents need to overcome a couple of denial issues regarding the extremely difficult topic of suicide:

- "It doesn't happen to kids like mine."

- "It only happens in faraway places."

- "My kids are immune from this."

- "The only kids who commit suicide are bad kids, horrible kids, kids from the other side of the tracks."

■ "This is not an issue I will ever have to deal with."

Teens and
Suicide

The incidence of suicide has, over the decades, shown one lone, tragic trend – up! Unfortunately, teenage suicide is not trending downward, so this problem has moved into the area of parenting for you and all of us.

Teenage mood swings include depression and a sense of hopelessness. Problem-solving skills are only beginning to emerge as children reach their teenage years. Youngsters working with their emotions are inexperienced, prone to exaggeration, and often easily give up. They have a hard time distinguishing between a disappointment and a disaster. If you don't believe me, just watch any three teenagers sitting down trying to solve an emotional problem together.

Don't role model the wrong things for your kids. You would be teaching your kids a very dangerous strategy.

Without intending to do so, parents can indirectly teach suicide by saying things like:

■ "Life is at best tedious."

■ "Life sucks."

■ "The world is no good anymore."

■ "The world is getting worse every day."

■ "I wish I didn't have to face the future."

■ "I don't want to live."

You need a value system that says suicide is not the last resort. You need a value system that says suicide is wrong. Very wrong.

To say that suicide is permissible under certain circumstances is to suggest to highly volatile human beings called teenagers that there might be circumstances in their very volatile lives where it should be considered as a viable option.

On the positive side, try to realize that parents have to be the light at the end of the tunnel for their kids. On the negative side, realize that depressed parents punish their children too often and too severely.

Depression

Kids get depressed. There are degrees of depression. It's sort of like injuries:

- There are little cuts that you can fix by putting a Band-Aid on them. So there are incidents of slight depression that a little cheering up will help a lot.

- Then there are bigger cuts, gashes, that require a visit to the emergency room. So, too, some forms of depression call for professional help.

There are conditions called "early onset mood disorders" which, if caught early enough, can be treated with remarkable results. If left untreated ("It's just a phase that 7-year-old Joey is going through"), great harm can be done. If you are in doubt, check with a highly skilled professional counselor or therapist.

And, please, don't punish your children for depression.

God and Suicide

Where do you find the rules against suicide to pass along to your children?

■ Would you go to the courthouse? Heavens no. Of course there are laws against suicide. But there is also a constant debate about these civil laws in the media and among various political groups.

■ Should we call the rules against suicide family values? No, don't do that either. To say "Our family is opposed to suicide" will appear to a teenager the same as "Our family doesn't like smoking."

■ Don't go to the law books or just to your family values. Go to a place where there is no debate. That's right. As parents, we need to turn to our religious code of morality.

So why is suicide wrong? Because God says so.

And why does God say so? For two reasons:

■ God says don't kill yourself because you are right now in a totally dark tunnel feeling totally hopeless. But it is a tunnel, and there is light at the end of it, and there God has waiting for you someone to give you light, to give you love, warmth, caring, sharing. And God doesn't want you to miss this gift of His. And He sure won't be happy if you miss the experience.

■ In addition, God put you on this earth to find the light at the end of the tunnel because He has sent you there to bring light, warmth, caring, sharing, and love to someone else. And He sure won't be happy if you don't show up for work. God says, "If you will take My hand, I will walk with you in the darkness and together we will walk to the dawn. I have been through the dark before. I know which way the dawn is. Grab My hand. Let's walk together."

Life is like a traffic jam on the Interstate. You are caught off guard, you are frustrated, the pace is slow, and it looks like "I'll never get out of here." But you do. And you have to remember that.

Warning Signs of Suicide

Be alert to the signs that your teen may be considering suicide. Notice that I didn't say watch for the signs. I said rather be alert for them. There is no sense filling your life with anxiety wondering whether signs of suicide will show up.

It simply means that you should be alert to when these basic patterns change in your child:

- Patterns of thinking.

- Patterns of feeling.

- Patterns of behavior.

Good parents have to be alert for signs of drug use. They have to be alert for signs of stealing. They have to be alert for signs of cheating in school.

A good shepherd isn't constantly worried about wolves attacking the sheep, but he always does have his early warning system up and operating.

Warning Signs

Here are 10 signs that should signal to you as a parent that there may be something wrong with your child:

1. Disruption in sleep patterns. A teen

may sleep much more than usual or be so nervous he or she prowls all night.

2. **Talking hopelessly about life** or being preoccupied with death.

3. **Change in the ways he or she spends time.** A gregarious kid holes up in his room. A stay-at-home goes out every night.

4. **Change in basic attitude.** Is a usually obedient child now challenging all the rules?

5. **Loss of interest in activities** he or she used to enjoy.

6. **Packing up or giving away treasured items** because "I won't need them anymore."

7. **Self-destructive actions** such as reckless driving, use of drugs or alcohol, or actual signs of suicide attempts such as slashes on the wrist.

8. **Evidence of a plan** such as a stash of pills or discovery of a hidden gun.

9. **Change in eating habits,** either overeating or near starvation.

10. **Anything that seems drastically out of the order** to you, the parent.

Dealing with a Friend's Suicide

What should your family do if a friend commits suicide?

This is at heart a teaching opportunity – a tragic but important time to bring the issue to the forefront.

To start with, let's stake out a middle ground for our family between spending too much time and too little time dealing with the issue, between obsessing every moment of every day to denial as if nothing happened.

This may be the first encounter for your child with death. It is most probably the first encounter for your child with the death of a peer.

Your child will be dealing with a series of unfamiliar, unhappy emotions, most of them pretty confusing. There are three areas to be looked at:

- *Behavior:* It's good for your child to spend time with classmates, but not too much. Day after day is way too much.

- *Feelings:* Feelings of loss are genuine and to be honored. Feelings of hopelessness are to be expressed, to be acknowledged, and then to be laid aside. There is always hope. Watch out for the fallacy: "I feel hopeless, therefore the situation is hopeless." That's called emotional thinking, letting our emotions control our thoughts. Remember that emotions are a notoriously unreliable guide if left unchecked.

- **_Thinking:_** This goes in two directions. The one direction is thinking of how discouraged the victim must have become to do this. How confused. How momentarily lost. How close to solutions at hand without reaching out for them. The other thoughts are about all the suffering that he brought into the world as a result of his suicide. All the pain to his family. All the hurt to his classmates. All the bad role-modeling. All the blessings he threw away. And the violation of God's good Commandments. That's right. The violation of God's good Commandments.

Whatever you do, please avoid making no one responsible: not you, not me, not the person himself. We live in an age of denial:

- It was nobody's fault.

- There was nothing we could do.

- That's just the way life is.

The biggest part of denial in our own age is to think of a suicide as similar to a little 8-year-old girl, in her First Communion dress and taking a flower to her grandmother, run over by a school bus. Suicide is not like that. Suicide also is:

- Not the same as a plane crash. No one chose to die in the plane crash.

- Not like cancer.

- Not a good choice. Never!

A person who commits suicide is a different kind of victim than this because it is voluntary and it is a choice. The person chose to take his or her own life.

What do you tell your children if a friend commits suicide? Here is what I say:

- I do not tell them he or she is in heaven.

- I do not tell them their friend is in hell.

- I tell them I do not know.

■ But I do tell them that God is very good and loving and merciful.

■ And I tell them we need to pray for their friend.

It needs to be stated very clearly that this advice is not for the family of the victim. It is for your family. Different words are needed for different situations.

One concluding thought: We are all concerned as parents about what is on TV. About our children learning the wrong things there. But I'll bet kids watch their parents more than they watch TV. They see their parents every day. The parent "show" runs around the clock. And they can't change the channel. So it really is important that *you* teach your children about this and other difficult topics.

Violence and *Children*

Moms and Dads worry a lot about their children. One of their biggest worries is violence. How do you help your son or daughter avoid being a victim or a victimizer? How do you teach your children to deal appropriately with anger and intimidation? Here are a few suggestions.

Don't Teach
Violence

Don't teach your children violence.

The basic principle here is: It is what you do as parents, not what the other person does that is most important.

There are not many really mean parents. But there are some. They beat their kids within an inch of their lives. They teach their children to do the same to the next generation.

Here is a typical example of how this kind of intergenerational violence is learned:

When I first met Mike, age 14, he was in a juvenile lockup. The night before, he had struck his mother repeatedly, breaking her jaw and two of her ribs. He told me that as a young boy of 4 or 5, he watched his father beat his mother repeatedly. Then Dad abandoned the family. Mike said, "Once I got big enough, I followed my father's example with my mother. He got his way by hitting her. I thought I could too."

If adults go around hitting people, screaming at them, shaking them, cursing, yelling, and hollering, their kids might think: "Dad gets his needs met that way, so maybe I can get my needs met that way too."

Horseplay and *Intimidation*

Much more common in many homes is horseplay. Sometimes horseplay is "just kidding around." But most of the time it is subtle intimidation.

Many, many fights among children start with innocent-looking horseplay. Simply don't tolerate it in your house, Mom and Dad, or in your school either.

Equally common is verbal intimidation which people use to get their way. By hurting people. By making them the butt of jokes. By sniping and carping.

Don't let this kind of behavior get a toe-hold in your house. The rule should be: "If you can't say something good, don't say anything at all."

Such behavior takes the warmth out of a home. Children feel unwelcome. They feel the coldness right away as soon as they enter. They have to constantly be on guard.

Also be careful of the engineers of violence whose basic premise is: "Let's get somebody else to fight." So they egg others on and then watch in glee as violence breaks out.

Managing *Violent* Impulses

It's good to ask whether violence is accepted in your family. What is its frequency and how do you react? Do these things happen in your home?

- Nonstop "nattering," criticism, and complaints.

- Constant insults.

- Too much rough horseplay.

- Violent outbursts.

- Throwing dishes.

- Smashing a window.

- Slugging a wall.

Help your children develop an attitude and spirit that are not fertile ground for violence. Think of all the children and adults who are successful in managing violent thoughts and impulses of their own and of others.

What are these people like?

■ They are honest and sensitive.

■ They love their kids and love their brothers and sisters.

■ They say their prayers every day.

■ They work out their frustrations and resentments appropriately through anger control techniques.

■ They are appropriately assertive so they can't be pushed around.

These skills and abilities can be learned. Just as you learned them, you can pass them on to your children.

People with a temper usually justify it by saying: "I was born with a temper." What they mean is that they do not intend to change and we should all learn to live with their terrible anger. That just doesn't seem fair.

On the other hand, you don't have to be a spoilsport either. Children need to learn the difference between violence in reality and fantasy. *America's Funniest Home Videos* is a good example. A person falls off the bleachers; nobody gets hurt. That's funny. But it isn't funny if people are badly hurt or die. That's gruesome. Children know that distinction and we can help reinforce it.

Self-Defense

What about teaching your children self-defense?

There are times when it is appropriate to defend yourself or your children. I know this seems like a gray area, and it doesn't seem much like a child's issue. Why? Because most children do tend to defend themselves when attacked.

The basic principle to remember is: Violence, even when legitimate, is a failure of everything else. It is giving up on negotiation, compromise, even flight, and it does have a price. Violence is not the first thing you should choose in self-defense and in defense of your children.

But it plays an important, yet minor role, especially in management of our fears. You shouldn't have to fear helplessly standing by and letting yourself or your children be beaten mercilessly. There is something you can do about it. That something even involves self-defense.

Remember: The best offense is a good defense.